TALK TO SOMEONE NOW

Questions on therapy, therapists,
and why we ALL have to open up.

Shaquille Joyce

TABLE OF CONTENTS

CHAPTER 3

2. Your Therapy Goals:
3. Everyday Stressors in Your Life
4. Subjects You Hesitate to Share with Others
5. Past Events Still Affecting You Today
6. Fears That Hold You Back
Reasons a therapist may not be the best for you
1. They're Not a Good Listener
2. They Downplay Your Feelings
3. You Don't Click with Them as a Person
4. You Don't Feel Safe
5. They Insult Your Intelligence
6. They Don't Encourage Personal Growth
7. Unethical Behavior
Ending Your Therapy
How to Break Up with Your Therapist Gracefully, according to a therapist
What Questions Should I Ask Myself Before Ending Therapy?
How Long Should I Give Therapy Before Deciding to Quit?
Should I Worry About Hurting My Therapist's Feelings if I Decide to Stop Seeing them?

CHAPTER 4

13 THERAPY TIPS FOR MAXIMIZING YOUR SESSIONS
1. Start with Admin Tasks
2. Let Your Emotions Flow
3. Keep the Focus on Yourself
4. Choose the Right Therapist
5. Build a Trusting Connection
6. Keep the Lines of Communication Open
7. Do Regular Check-Ins
8. Don't Stick Around in an Unfulfilling Relationship
9. Seek Out Recurring Themes and Patterns
10. Share the Uncomfortable Thoughts

11. Embrace Change and Be Ready for It
12. Extend the Work Beyond Your Sessions
13. Embrace the Journey
What to not say to your therapist
1. "I Agree with You Completely."
2. "That's What You Would Have Done, right?"
3.   "Tell Me What I Should Do."

CHAPTER 5

WHEN IS IT TIME TO END THERAPY?
Starting with the End in Mind
Recognizing the Signs of Closure
Are You Ready to Say Goodbye?

CONCLUSION

EMBRACING THE BEAUTY OF THERAPY

Introduction

Lately, it seems like mental health and well-being are the talk of the town. What used to be hush-hush or considered a no-go zone is now something folks are sharing openly. People are coming forward to talk about their experiences and what they go through behind closed doors, all in the hope of helping others.

These days, you'll find more and more chatter about the importance of mental health and therapy. It's become so common that chances are someone in your social circle is either openly or quietly seeing a therapist. This shift in conversation is a good thing because it's pushing more people to get the help they need from therapists and counselors. These professionals can guide individuals on their journey to becoming happier, healthier, and more balanced.

Still, the idea of seeking therapy can be a bit intimidating if you're new to it. If you've heard about therapy and are curious about how it could benefit your life, keep reading. I am here to shed some light on what therapy can do for you.

What is therapy?

What exactly is therapy, you might wonder? Well, therapy, often referred to as talk therapy, is when you, your family, or even as a couple, sit down with a therapist, licensed clinical social worker, or another mental health pro. It's all about getting some support in your life and relationships.

People turn to therapy for all sorts of reasons. It could be a big life event, tangled-up relationships, or personal challenges they're dealing with. The beauty of therapy is that it's a safe and confidential space where you can unpack your experiences and feelings. You've got a supportive, neutral person right there to help you make sense of it all. Plus, your therapist can arm you with some nifty tools to handle everything in the healthiest way possible.

Therapists have a bunch of different approaches to help with your unique needs. Each therapist has their own specialties, but they're trained in various methods and can team up with you to pick the path that suits you best.

Chapter 1
When Should You Start Therapy?

You were wondering when's the right time to start therapy? Well, here's the truth: there is no general answer for everyone. Therapy is there for you, no matter what's going on in your life, where you stand, or how you got there. You don't need a specific reason or some magic "right time" to give it a shot. It's entirely up to you, whenever you feel it's necessary.

People need therapy for all types of reasons. From breakdowns in communication to dealing with the loss of a loved one and everything in between, life throws various challenges our way.

Some of the most common reasons folks begin therapy include things like battling addiction or substance abuse, wrestling with anxiety and depression, coping with grief and loss, managing chronic illnesses, mood and eating disorders, self-esteem issues, handling phobias and OCD, or recovering from trauma.

The bottom line is that therapy can work wonders in many of life's situations. So, if any of the conditions mentioned above sound familiar to you, it might be a great idea to reach out to a mental health pro and start your therapy journey.

Therapy can be incredibly beneficial in addressing these and many other life circumstances. If you or someone you know is dealing with any of the above conditions, consider reaching out to a mental health professional to start the therapy process.

Types of Therapy

When it comes to therapy, again it's not a one-size-fits-all approach. Therapists are trained in various models and practices because what works well for one person might not have the same impact on another. That's why it's essential to consult a professional who can help steer you in the direction that's most effective for your healing journey.

If you're not a licensed therapist, the world of therapy models can seem foreign and unfamiliar. While you don't need to be an expert in every type of psychotherapy, it can be beneficial to have a basic understanding of some of the common approaches used by mental health professionals.

Here are some of the most frequently employed types of therapy:

- Cognitive Behavioral Therapy (CBT)
- Dialectical Behavioral Therapy (DBT)
- Emotionally Focused Therapy (EFT)
- Eye Movement Desensitization and Reprocessing (EMDR)
- Internal Family Systems (IFS)

These practices represent just a handful of the many therapeutic approaches available today, you can always dive in to research about each approach on your own, as that is not really the focus of this material, so let us continue.

Benefits of Therapy

Alright, let's get real about the perks of therapy – it's not just about venting and having someone nod along. Therapy goes way beyond that, and it can seriously level up your life inside and out.

❖ Boosted Coping Skills

Life can be a wild rollercoaster, right? It's not all sunshine and rainbows; there are plenty of tough moments too. Now, it's not like we're born with a magical set of coping skills. Sure, our folks do their best, but most of us could use a bit more in our toolkit. Therapy is like going to a coping skills workshop. Your therapist helps you discover and build those essential skills. Think of it as upgrading your toolbox with more tools. So, when life throws those curveballs, you've got what it takes to handle them like a champ.

❖ Unpacking Past Experiences and Traumas

Our life story shapes who we are. But if you haven't had a therapist by your side from day one, there's a good chance you're carrying some emotional baggage from the past. Childhood traumas, family dynamics, losses, or any kind of abuse – all of that stuff needs to be unpacked. Therapy is like your emotional storage unit. Through various methods, your therapist helps you process and let go of that heavy stuff.

Plus, tackling your past can be a game-changer. It can prevent messed-up relationships, mental health hiccups, addiction, and those never-ending toxic cycles with your loved ones. Facing these experiences in a healthy way can unlock your potential to thrive in life.

❖ Building Better Self-Esteem and Self-Worth

You know what? More people wrestle with self-esteem issues than we might think. It's not just about physical insecurities; many folks go through life without feeling really good about themselves. If you're one of them, it's not your fault – it can come from a bunch of things. Your therapist is like a personal self-discovery guide, helping you peel back those layers that might be holding you back. Whether it's past trauma, losing yourself in a relationship, or feeling uneasy about your body, your therapist can help you process these experiences and get to the heart of who you really are. When you reconnect with your true self, heal old wounds, and kick those insecurities to the curb, you can step into a world of confidence and a strong sense of self.

❖ Improved Emotion Management

Picture those moments when your patience gets tested or someone or something really gets under your skin. How do you typically react? Do you lose your cool, shout, internalize it, or stay cool as a cucumber? There's no right or wrong here, and you're definitely not broken based on how you respond. But there's a big difference between reacting and responding.

Reacting is like your knee-jerk reaction, just doing what feels natural without much thought. Therapy can help you spot the quirks in how you handle uncomfortable or triggering situations. It's like getting an emotional toolkit upgrade. Your therapist can equip you with tools to respond differently.

When you respond, you're taking a step back, using your smarts, and your fancy tools to deal with the tough stuff without making things worse. So, instead of getting all hot-headed or impulsive, you could eventually tackle those triggers in a calm and productive way that actually leads to resolutions and peace.

❖ **Healthier and More Effective Communication**

Now, let's talk about something therapy is famous for – improving how we communicate. So many of our relationship issues boil down to not getting our message across effectively. It's like trying to win a game with the wrong rulebook.

If you grew up in an environment where healthy communication and conflict resolution were about as common as a unicorn, you might feel like you're on the losing side of the relationship battle as an adult. The thing is, we often mirror the way we were spoken to as kids, which can be a mixed bag depending on your family background but the great news is that in therapy, you get a chance to break those old patterns and rewrite your communication story. Therapists can work their magic in couples or family sessions, guiding everyone to communicate more effectively. Plus, they can also work with you one-on-one to improve how you communicate outside of those relationships.

In therapy, you'll learn some valuable communication skills like how to listen and receive others' words calmly, express your feelings in a way that others can understand, tackle conversations with the goal of finding resolutions, and even fight fairly. You'll also pick up some language tools, like using "I feel" statements.

Effective communication is a journey, It takes time and effort, especially since you often have to unlearn old habits. But if you and your loved ones are up for putting in the work, the benefits can be pretty darn amazing.

❖ **Managing Symptoms of Mental Health Conditions**

Many folks who seek therapy either have a mental health diagnosis or suspect they're dealing with some kind of mental illness. Depending on your condition and how it's affecting you, therapy might be just one piece of the puzzle. In some cases, you might need to team up with a psychiatric provider for things like medication management. In other situations, therapy alone might be the right path.

The key here is to connect with a professional who can help you figure out the best treatment plan for your unique situation. But no matter what, talk therapy can be a valuable tool in managing the symptoms of mental illness. It can work alongside other treatments or be a standalone method.

Therapists have specific techniques tailored to help with various mental health conditions, whether it's mood disorders, depression, anxiety, personality disorders, or other common issues. They'll guide you through managing your thoughts, emotions, actions, and symptoms in a way that makes your life healthier and more functional.

12 Signs It's Time to Chat with a Therapist

You know, there are the common reasons people seek therapy, some of which we mentioned above, but there are also some less talked about behaviors and thoughts that might be nudging you toward a therapist's office. So, let's dive into 12 questions to help you figure out if it's time for a chat with a therapist.

1. Feeling Misunderstood?

Ever get the feeling that nobody really gets you? It's not uncommon for teenagers to go through this phase, but if you're well into your late 20s or beyond and still feel like an enigma to the world, it could be related to intimacy, identity, or communication issues. These things often trace back to our upbringing or childhood traumas, making it a good reason to talk to a therapist. Sometimes, if your perspective on the world is consistently at odds with everyone else, it might be a sign of a personality disorder.

2. Relationship Hiccups After 30?

Are you over 30 but can't seem to keep a relationship going for more than six months? It could be a fear of intimacy or some sneaky relationship patterns you're not even aware of. A therapist can help you see the problem clearly and provide a safe space to work on trust issues. If you find yourself falling in love like clockwork but it fizzles out after a few months or if your relationships are like a constant push-and-pull, it might also be a sign of borderline personality disorder. In such cases, talking to a therapist can be a game-changer.

3. Perpetual Fatigue?

Do you always feel tired, no matter how much you sleep? If the doctor has given you a clean bill of health, it might be time for some therapy. Constant fatigue can actually be a sneaky sign of depression. Sometimes there's something bothering you more than you realize, and addressing it might be the key to regaining your energy.

4. Notorious Impulsivity?

We all have our spontaneous moments, but if your impulsivity tends to wreck your relationships or career, it's more than just a quirky trait. High impulsivity is often linked to a history of childhood trauma and can be a prominent symptom of borderline personality disorder.

5. Stuck in an Unhappy Relationship?

Feeling trapped in a relationship you're not thrilled about? This could be a sign of low self-worth or codependency. These deep-rooted patterns can be tough to change without some support. The longer you stay, the more your self-esteem can plummet, potentially leading to depression.

6. Mysterious Physical Symptoms?

Dealing with ongoing physical symptoms that leave your family doctor scratching their head? For some, it might be persistent muscle tension or sleep troubles, indicating underlying anxiety or depression. Others may experience unexplained recurring medical symptoms that seem to have a mental root. While it's not fully understood why mental struggles sometimes manifest as physical symptoms, talking to a therapist can't hurt and might even improve your physical well-being.

7. Pessimistic Outlook?

Do you have a knack for thinking life is just meant to be tough and you're forever unlucky? If your thoughts lean toward the negative, often veering into extremes, and you're experiencing a constant cloud of doom and gloom, negative thinking might be the culprit. This negative thinking can lead to a cycle of low moods and poor life choices, keeping you stuck in a downward spiral. Cognitive behavioral therapy (CBT) can help break this cycle and teach you the art of balanced thinking. It's like finding a window you didn't know existed.

8. Recently Moved Country?

Sure, moving to a new country may sound thrilling at first, but then reality hits, and you might feel lonely, lost, and totally disconnected. Well, you're not alone if you feel this way. Moving to a different country can trigger anxiety, and depression, and even put a strain on relationships if you've moved as a couple or a family. If you've been struggling with these feelings for a few months or more, it's a perfectly valid reason to reach out to a therapist.

9. Saying Yes When You Mean No?

Do you find it difficult to say no? Are you constantly drained from doing things you're not really interested in, all because you can't turn people down? Or perhaps you're stuck in relationships you're not keen on because you don't know how to let someone down gently. It's a clear sign that personal boundaries might be a bit blurry for you. Changing this pattern isn't a piece of cake, but a therapist can help you understand why this happens and guide you in reclaiming your personal power.

10.　　World Feels Dangerous?

Do you often feel like the world is a very dangerous place, and it's not just because of something you read in the news or a bad experience? This pervasive feeling of danger often stems from a strong negative core belief, typically rooted in childhood trauma. Left untreated, it can hold you back from reaching your full potential or sabotage the good things in life just to prove your belief true.

11.　　Nighttime Heart Pounding?

Do you wake up in the middle of the night and feel your heart racing? Well, some medical conditions, like menopause, can play a role, but if your doctor gives you a clean bill of health, it could be what's known as night anxiety. Some of us manage to keep our anxiety in check during the day, but it creeps up on us at night. The good news is that treating the anxiety can put an end to those sleepless nights.

12.　　Hating Your Job?

Sure, many of us endure jobs we're not wild about while we pave the way for our future. But if you've consistently found yourself in jobs you despise, it might not just be the way life is. Deep down, it could be a lack of confidence or a fear of upsetting others that's keeping you stuck. Talk therapies can be incredibly useful for workplace issues, helping you figure out what you genuinely want and take those steps toward change.

Chapter 2
Differences Between Therapy and Talking to Your Friends

Now, let's chat about how talking to a therapist differs from sharing with a friend or family member. You might be wondering if it's worth your time and money. After all, what's the real benefit of those therapy sessions?

These are all excellent questions, often fueled by uncertainty. You might have friends and family to talk to, which is great, but there usually comes a point where you realize you need something more.

The thing is, talking to a therapist goes beyond just chatting. It's a journey of self-discovery, uncovering aspects of yourself and your behaviors that often stay hidden. These are things that can significantly impact your daily life, and it takes a skilled listener to help you navigate through them. So, when you're ready to dig deeper, that's where therapy truly shines.

Having a Chat vs. Therapy: What Sets Them Apart

Let's talk about the difference between having a casual conversation and the power of therapy. It's crucial to understand that the two have unique roles in our lives:

Therapist vs. Friend Support:

A therapist listens to your story and supports you based on your goals. They won't impose their own solutions; it's all about what's right for you. On the other hand, friends might offer support based on what they would do in your shoes, well-intentioned but not always aligned with your needs.

Flow and Interruptions:

In therapy, there's a flow. Therapists know when to let you speak, when silence is golden, and when to challenge gently. They won't interrupt your thoughts. Friends, however, might jump in with their thoughts, often to make you feel better or because they care deeply.

It's All About You:

Therapy is your time, consistent and structured. It's a process focused solely on you. Friendships are a two-way street. Sometimes, you might go around in circles, discussing the same things repeatedly.

Empathy and Sharing:

Therapists empathize with your experiences and aim to understand your perspective. Friends might try to connect by sharing their own experiences. While this is well-intentioned, it can inadvertently make you feel guilty for feeling the way you do.

Questioning and Exploration:

Therapists ask skillful questions to help you uncover essential aspects of your experiences. They pinpoint those crucial words that reveal core beliefs for deeper exploration. Friends may not have this capacity.

Non-Judgmental Space:

Therapists offer a non-judgmental zone because they don't know your history or the people you're discussing. Friends and family, despite their best intentions, might inadvertently judge or offer opinions.

Reflection and Summary:

Therapists summarize and reflect on what you've shared, not just in one session but over time. They identify patterns to offer clarity. Friends tend to keep the conversation moving forward.

Safety and Confidentiality:

Therapists provide a safe and confidential environment. What you share in therapy stays there. It's hard to find this level of trust elsewhere. Can you really trust your friends, colleagues, and family to keep your secrets?

- **Skills and Experience:**

Therapists bring skills and experience from working with various clients and ongoing supervision. They can offer insights from a wealth of knowledge. Friends may not have this level of expertise, but their support is from the heart.

Navigating Relationships: Friends vs. Therapists

You know, relationships with friends and family can get pretty tangled. Sometimes, they might not want you to change because they're getting something out of the way things are. But here's the deal: a therapist is all about helping you become the person you want to be.

1. *The Power of a Dedicated Listener:*
A therapist is like your personal detective for those tiny nuances in your voice or subtle gestures you might not

even notice. They can make a world of difference when they point these out.

2. *Unpacking Unhealthy Patterns:*

Therapists are like strategy wizards. They'll guide you in spotting those sneaky unhealthy thinking patterns and behaviors. But here's the catch—it takes time. Do your friends have the time and expertise to support you like this?

3. *Personalized Support:*

Therapists truly dedicate themselves to your journey. They listen, they guide, and they're committed to helping you transform. It's not something your friends can fully replace.

Here's the bottom line: our friends, colleagues, and family are an essential part of our lives, offering support, connection, and a place to vent. But they can't give you the luxury of undivided attention, the time to dive deep into your thoughts and feelings, or the opportunity to truly understand yourself on a conscious level.

Therapy, on the other hand, is a game-changer. It empowers you, changes lives, and sometimes even saves them. While our nearest and dearest play a vital role, when you need to focus on yourself, it's time to talk to a qualified, skilled, and experienced counselor. Trust me, it's a unique experience. Choosing the Right Therapist: Your Personal Journey

The Quest for the Perfect Therapist:

Let's talk about something super important—finding the right therapist. You see, it's a bit like dating; you want to connect with someone whose personality and approach feel just right for you.

Picking the right therapist can be a real challenge. After all, what you're dealing with is deeply personal stuff. And you've got a bunch of options when it comes to mental health professionals.

Lynn Bufka, Ph.D., a licensed clinical psychologist and an expert at the American Psychological Association, puts it this way: "Your job is to find somebody who maps onto the concerns you have, somebody you feel comfortable with, and somebody who you believe will be helpful and supportive to you."

The Perfect Match:

You're after someone who's not only a pro at tackling your specific issues but also someone you can vibe with. And here's the kicker—they need to be available, accepting new clients, and budget-friendly.

 Research tells us that the relationship between you and your therapist is a massive deal. A strong connection, feeling like you're on the same wavelength, and collaborating together are what makes therapy work its magic.

In fact, a bunch of studies involving over 30,000 patients found that this connection is just as important as the type of therapy you get.

So, the big question is, how do you find your mental health match made in heaven?

What type of therapist do you need?

First things first, you've taken a big step by deciding you want to talk to someone about your mental and emotional well-being. Now, it's time to figure out what you want to discuss, your goals for therapy, and what kind of therapist you need.

You've got plenty of options, from psychiatrists to psychologists to social workers and counselors. But not all of them can diagnose mental conditions or prescribe medication. Also, each type has different areas of expertise.

For instance, if you're wrestling with trust issues or relationship problems, a marriage counselor might be your go-to. On the other hand, if you're dealing with substance abuse, divorce, or family turmoil, family therapy could be just the thing.

Remember, it's your journey, and finding the right therapist is a big part of making it a successful one. So, take your time, do some research, and you'll be on the path to personal growth and well-being.

Your Personal Guide to Finding the Right Therapist

Alright, now that you've figured out the type of therapist you need, it's time to find the perfect one in your area. Here are a few tips to help you start.

1. Get a Referral:

First, reach out to people you trust, like your doctor or a family member. You'd be surprised how often they can point you in the right direction. In fact, a survey found that 39 percent of folks who sought therapy got a referral from their primary care physician, and 19 percent received a recommendation from a friend. Even if you don't think you need medical treatment, talking to your doctor about your symptoms is a smart move. They can help you figure out the best type of provider for your needs.

2. Use Online Databases:

Several mental health organizations have handy databases of licensed therapists. You can search for professionals by location, so you can find someone nearby. These databases often let you filter your results based on factors like gender or whether you want in-person or online counseling.

3. Check with Your Insurance:

If you have health insurance, call your provider to get a list of mental health professionals in your network. This way, you can find therapists in your area who accept your insurance plan. It's a budget-friendly way to get the support you need.

4. Explore Online Therapy Platforms:

Online therapy platforms are pretty cool because they let you easily switch therapists until you find the perfect match.

What About Culturally Competent Providers?

Sometimes, you're looking for a therapist who gets where you're coming from, whether it's a shared background or specific challenges like dealing with a chronic illness or disability. You can also reach out to organizations like the Association of Black Psychologists, the Asian Mental Health Collective, or the Hispanic Access Foundation for referrals.

Remember, there's no one-size-fits-all solution when it comes to therapy. You've got the power to find someone who truly understands and supports you. It's all about finding the right fit for your unique journey.

Finding the correct Therapist for Your Particular Needs

Now, let's get even more specific about finding a therapist who specializes in the exact conditions or concerns you have. There are organizations out there that can help you in this process. They either have directories of therapists or can give you referrals. Here are some of these helpful organizations in the United States:

Anxiety Disorders of America

Autism Society of America

Depression and Bipolar Support Alliance

International OCD Foundation

Psychology Today OCD Therapist Locator

Once you've got some names or a list, how do you pick the right one?

Here's how to narrow down your options:

1. *Check Their Credentials:*

First things first, ensure that the therapists on your shortlist are properly qualified. Most therapists will proudly display their licenses, degrees, and certifications (like Ph.D., MD, or LCSW) on their websites. But if you can't find this information, don't hesitate to ask. You can also check the licensing status of any mental health professional in your state via the licensing board or whichever organization is responsible for that in your nation.

2. *Consider Their Areas of Expertise:*

What do you need help with? if you are grieving the loss of a loved one or dealing with family conflicts or substance abuse, Check if the therapists on your list specialize in the areas you need assistance with. Some therapists focus on specific conditions such as PTSD, depression, anxiety, phobias, or panic disorders, while others may specialize in grief, substance abuse, or other issues. The key here is that counseling should align with what you want to address – it's your journey, your call.

3.Explore Their Treatment Approaches:

Therapists use various therapeutic techniques to help their clients. For example, if you're dealing with persistent negative thoughts affecting your daily life, cognitive behavioral therapy (CBT) might be the way to go. This type of therapy is designed to help you change your thought patterns and behaviors. If you're tackling a phobia, exposure therapy could be a good fit. If you have a particular treatment method in mind, check if your prospective provider is trained in it and offers it. Do a Quick Google Search:

Many therapists have websites or online profiles that can give you a sense of their experience and expertise. Take a look to see if they resonate with you.

4. Set Up a Screening Call:

Consider arranging a 10-minute screening call to get to know your potential therapist. The goal is to determine if you feel comfortable talking to them if they can address your specific issues, and if their therapeutic style works for you. Just call the provider's office and ask if they offer screener interviews or initial introductory chats to help you determine if they're a good fit. Some additional questions you might want to ask are:

"Can you prescribe medication if I need it, or can you refer me to someone who can?"

Helping Yourself Along the Recovery Journey

So, you're considering therapy, but you might have some questions in mind. That's perfectly normal! Here are a few things you might want to know:

How Can I Play a Role in My Own Recovery?

Taking an active role in your recovery is a great approach. You can make the most out of therapy by being open and honest with your therapist. If there's something specific you want to address, let them know. Remember, therapy is a collaborative process and your input matters.

When Will I Start Feeling Better?

It's natural to wonder when you'll start feeling the effects of therapy. But then, there's no one answer to this question. The timeframe varies depending on individual circumstances, goals, and the type of therapy you're receiving. It's something you can discuss with your therapist to set realistic expectations.

What If I Don't Feel Better in the Usual Timeframe?

While there may be a typical timeframe for progress, everyone's journey is unique. If you find that you're not experiencing the improvements you anticipated, it's essential to communicate this with your therapist. They can adjust the approach, discuss any challenges you're facing, and guide you through it.

Additional Practical Aspects to Consider When Choosing a therapist

Besides the therapy itself, there are some logistical details that deserve your attention during the decision-making process. These include:

Costs: Can you comfortably manage the fees your therapist charges for each session? It's a crucial point to clarify, and you should inquire about available payment options. Some therapists offer sliding pay scales to make therapy more affordable for those with lower incomes.

Availability: Make sure the therapists on your list are taking on new clients. Sometimes, you might be placed on a waitlist. During your initial contact, inquire about when you can start your sessions.

Accessibility: If you prefer remote therapy through platforms like Zoom rather than commuting to a therapist's office, prioritize providers who offer telemedicine services.

Proximity: For those who lean towards in-person counseling or like the option of visiting a therapist's office, consider therapists in your local area. Think about practical factors such as parking, traffic during rush hours, and the therapist's office hours when evaluating your choices.

Chapter 3
What Really Happens During a Therapy Session?

What really goes on in a therapy session?

So, you might be wondering,

Well, the answer is: it depends! Let us explore it together, shall we?

What's My Role in a Therapy Session?

In a therapy session, your role is pretty simple. You share what's on your mind, what's bothering you, or what you're feeling. It's your space to open up about your thoughts and emotions. The structure can vary based on the type of therapy, whether it's one-on-one or in a group, and the specific issue you're dealing with. Sometimes, you might work through exercises designed to tackle your specific concern, while in other sessions, you may have a more general chat about how you're doing.

What Kind of Questions Will They Ask Me?

Your therapist might ask all sorts of questions depending on what you're seeking help for and the type of therapy you're receiving. It could be about your relationships, your childhood, your emotions, your thoughts, or even certain situations or events that you find challenging. The idea is to get a better understanding of what's going on in your life.

How Long Are These Sessions?

Therapy sessions come in different flavors when it comes to duration. They can range from a quick 30 minutes to a lengthy hour and a half, with the most common session lasting about 50 minutes. The length can depend on your specific therapy type, your issue, and how you're feeling. Group sessions may run a bit longer than individual ones.

How Often Will I Be in Therapy?

The frequency of your therapy sessions varies. You might have weekly sessions or even meet with your therapist two or three times a week. The type of therapy, your access to treatment, and your own well-being can influence the schedule. When you're not feeling your best, you might see your therapist more often.

Is Therapy on the Right Track?

After a few sessions, it's a good sign if you feel like therapy, is a collaborative effort. If you and your therapist have a good working relationship and you both feel engaged, that's promising. But if you're feeling stuck, uncertain about the direction, or disconnected, don't hesitate to discuss this with your therapist. It's not just about discussing external problems; building a strong therapeutic alliance can also enhance your mental well-being. So, keep the communication flowing

Getting the Most Out of Therapy

Therapy can sometimes be quite a rollercoaster. You might have moments when you wonder if your psychologist is a bit distant or you're not on the same page. If you're feeling this way, don't hesitate to bring it up. It's important to discuss any concerns or disagreements about the therapy process. And if you ever find yourself tempted to cancel or end your sessions, it's crucial to let your psychologist know. If you feel progress is slower than you'd like, that's another thing to discuss.

During therapy, people go through a range of emotions. You might be worried about delving into painful experiences, and that's perfectly okay. No one will force you to discuss things you're not ready for. But when you do feel comfortable talking about these issues, it's a sign that you're building trust in the therapeutic relationship and making strides in understanding your distress.

Remember, therapy is no walk in the park; it's challenging and requires effort. Delving into difficult feelings and thoughts is tough work. It also takes time to establish trust and comfort within the therapeutic relationship.

What If Things Aren't Getting Better?

If you've already discussed your concerns with your therapist, but you're not seeing improvement, it might be a good idea to ask your therapist or your GP for a referral to someone else.

Maximizing Your Therapy Session:

You really want to make the most of your sessions?

Forget the Clock: Allow your therapist to manage the session time. Focus totally on yourself for that period of time.

Integrate It into Life: Apply what you learn in therapy to other aspects of your life. The true benefits come when you use these insights beyond the therapy room.

Relationship Matters: If you have any concerns about your relationship with your therapist, don't hesitate to bring them up. Your collaboration with your therapist greatly influences the success of your therapy goals.

Ask Freely: You can ask anything you want. There's no need to hold back; your therapist will clarify their boundaries. Your therapy hour is your space to be your authentic self.

Curiosity is Key: Embrace the inquisitive mindset in therapy. Wonder why you reacted a certain way to an innocent question or why you got upset when your colleague commented on your shirt. Real change comes with understanding.

Seek Clarification: Don't hesitate to ask your therapist to explain if you don't understand something. Therapists can sometimes forget that not everyone is familiar with psychological jargon.

Go Deeper: If you're just chatting without a clear direction, pause and talk about how you feel the therapy isn't progressing. Dedicate your session to exploring your feelings, thoughts, and behaviors.

Embrace Change: Change can be intimidating because it's unfamiliar. Even if your current situation is causing distress, it might feel safer because it's known. But sometimes, it's worth the risk. Mental health challenges don't vanish on their own; they require your active involvement. Therapy is your opportunity to understand the root of your issues and work toward a happier, healthier life.

What to Discuss in Your Therapy Session

Congratulations on taking that big step to prioritize your mental well-being by starting therapy. It's perfectly normal to wonder what to talk about during your sessions. The first therapy appointment often follows a certain structure, usually beginning with an intake evaluation. Michele Goldman, a psychologist and media advisor for the Hope for Depression Research Foundation, explains this typically covers your work, relationships, medical and mental health history, and more.

Once you've got the basics out of the way, the sky's the limit when it comes to what you can talk about. There's no right or wrong subject. The time is yours, so you choose how you use it. If you feel a need to speak about something, then that is something you should talk about. There is no topic that is off limits."

But if you're feeling a bit lost about where to begin, here are a few ideas to get the conversation flowing:

1.   *What Led You to Seek Therapy:*
You didn't decide to see a therapist on a whim. There was something that made you take this important step, start there. Discuss why you're in therapy and maybe explore what held you back from seeking help before. Share the details of what brought you to therapy.

2. *Your Therapy Goals:*
Your goals for therapy may be related to why you sought help, but they might be different too. Consider what changes you'd like to see in your life after several months of therapy. Discussing your vision of success in therapy can be quite helpful. It not only provides you with direction but also helps you and your therapist work toward a common goal. Whether it's healing from a breakup or finding a way to move forward when you feel stuck, let your therapist in on what you hope to achieve.

3. Everyday Stressors in Your Life

Life can be full of stress, and sometimes it's good to talk about it with a neutral party. Venting and unloading your stress can be helpful, but it goes beyond that. Discussing stressors in therapy can also lead to problem-solving. Your therapist might offer different ways to tackle those stressors. Starting with a story about your stressful relationship with your mom is a bit easier than diving straight into analyzing your entire life's journey.

4. Subjects You Hesitate to Share with Others

Even if you're close to your partner and friends, there are probably certain things you're reluctant to discuss with them. This is where your therapist comes in. Whether it's awkward questions, topics that fill you with shame, or painful memories from the past, these are all worth exploring in therapy. If you've been avoiding discussing something for some reason, therapy can be a safe space to confront it.

5. Past Events Still Affecting You Today

No matter who we are, we all have past events that left a mark on us. If you find yourself continually thinking about these past experiences, it might be a good idea to delve into them in therapy. Talking about the past can help resolve lingering feelings and shed light on any present issues they might be causing.

6. Fears That Hold You Back

Fear is a common human experience, and it can often hold us back. Whether it's fear of vulnerability, fear of unearthing deep emotions, or fear of revisiting old wounds, these are all valid topics to explore in therapy. Many of us have fears that prevent us from living our best lives, and therapy can be a place to address and overcome these fears.

Reasons a therapist may not be the best for you

Remember we said therapy is a bit like a relationship? Sometimes this person is not just who you should be with and that goes for therapy too. Here are a few reasons why your therapist may not be the best for you.

1. They're Not a Good Listener

Your first session with a therapist should focus on what brought you there in the first place. If you notice your therapist not really paying attention, looking at their phone, or doing more talking than listening, it's a red flag. Your time and money are valuable, and you shouldn't have to struggle to get your point across.

2. They Downplay Your Feelings

Validating your emotions is crucial for effective therapy. If your therapist dismisses or downplays your concerns, it's a sign that they might not be the right fit for you. Your feelings should be taken seriously.

3. You Don't Click with Them as a Person

It might sound trivial, but liking your therapist as a person is important. As Dr. Tarik Shaheen puts it, you should build a strong and valuable relationship with your therapist while working toward your goals. In simpler terms, you should genuinely like your therapist. If you don't, it could affect the results you're hoping to achieve.

4. You Don't Feel Safe

A therapist should create a safe environment where you can discuss anything. If you feel unable to share your innermost thoughts, ask yourself why. If it's because you're not ready to address certain issues, that's okay. However, if it's because the therapist makes you uncomfortable, it's time to look for someone else. Therapists must establish trust by maintaining boundaries and not making you feel uneasy.

5. They Insult Your Intelligence

Regardless of their expertise, you know your struggles better than anyone. Therapists should not belittle your experiences. If you mention a method that helps you and they dismiss it, consider whether they're truly focused on your well-being or if they're too fixated on their preferred approach.

6. They Don't Encourage Personal Growth

The duration of therapy varies, but it's essential that you see progress. If you're stuck in endless sessions with no improvement in sight, it might be time to find a therapist who challenges you more. While some people need ongoing support, many can recover and lead happier lives. If you're not benefitting from the therapy, discuss your options with your therapist or consider going a different route.

7. Unethical Behavior

Therapists have a strict code of ethics to follow. They can't form friendships or romantic relationships with their patients, and they must keep your information confidential. While it might be tough to part ways with a therapist you don't have personal issues with, remember that your mental health should come first.

Ending Your Therapy

Telling your therapist that you won't be returning can feel empowering, or it can be a bit intimidating. Whether you decide to have an open conversation with them or slowly fade away, what really matters is looking out for your mental well-being. If your therapist shows any of the seven signs mentioned earlier, it's probably time for a change.

How to Break Up with Your Therapist Gracefully, according to a therapist

Breaking up can be tough, but what about calling it quits on your therapist? If your therapy sessions aren't quite hitting the mark or you're just ready to move on, you might be wondering how to navigate this change gracefully.

Think about your last heart-to-heart with your best friend. You probably spilled your thoughts, felt completely open, and valued their input. That's how your therapist's office should feel too. Therapist, Irina Fierstein explains, "You and your therapist are a good fit if you believe they truly understand you. Their insights are helpful, and you can tell they are engaged because they work with the feedback you provide. If you feel at ease with them and sense a connection during your sessions, you're more likely to leave with advice that's genuinely beneficial for your life and your therapy goals."

But if you find yourself holding back in sessions or you don't click with your therapist in a way that makes you comfortable, it might be time to consider parting ways.

What Questions Should I Ask Myself Before Ending Therapy?

Remember, therapy is a two-way street. While not every therapist will be a perfect match for every patient, it's crucial to take a look inside and ensure you're putting in your best effort before deciding to move on.

 Before concluding your therapist isn't right for you, you should be honest with yourself. Ask questions like, **'Am I motivated to put in the work for therapy? Am I openly sharing any negative feelings I have about these sessions? What precisely isn't working for me, and do I know what changes I'm looking for?'** Once you've figured out your answers, you're ready to start discussing your feelings with your therapist.

How Long Should I Give Therapy Before Deciding to Quit?

There's no strict rule about how many sessions you should commit to with a new therapist before determining if it's a good fit. It could be a gut feeling after the first meeting or maybe after a month of treatment. But you'll likely know when it's just not working out.

 If you feel an immediate negative vibe, there's no need for a second session. If you're uncertain, share your feelings with your therapist and see how they handle it. They might encourage you both to open up and explore your connection more deeply. If you've given it a fair shot and still feel it's not the right fit, it's time to move on.

Should I Worry About Hurting My Therapist's Feelings if I Decide to Stop Seeing them?

Therapists are trained to help us address our mental and emotional struggles. But sometimes, despite everyone's best intentions, it doesn't click. And that's okay. If your therapist isn't helping you, He/she doesn't want to waste your time or theirs.

You don't need to worry about hurting your therapist's feelings if you both decide it's not a good fit. While it's possible that the therapist may feel something, it's everyone's responsibility to reflect on what went wrong when a patient decides to move on. As the patient, your primary concern should be yourself. Remember, you're also a client in this relationship, and if you're not getting what you need, there's no need to fret. How to Tell Your Therapist You're Ending the Relationship

Breaking the news can feel daunting, but it's best to rip off the Band-Aid. If you've made up your mind to seek a new therapist, it's important to inform your current one as soon as possible. Just be honest and straightforward.

keep it simple, saying something like, "I think I need a different approach," or "I believe we've gone as far as we can together." Sometimes, patients avoid the conversation and opt not to schedule another appointment, or they might say, "Work is too hectic right now." And that's okay! You don't need to feel overwhelmed when ending a therapy relationship.

Remember, every therapist has been through this before, so there's no need to stress. A good therapist will handle it professionally and genuinely wish you the best.

Chapter 4

13 Therapy Tips for Maximizing Your Sessions

Deciding to start therapy is a significant step, and it involves a substantial commitment of your time, emotions, and often your finances. It's only natural to want to ensure that you're making the most of this investment. it's essential to approach your sessions with an open mind and a willingness to put in the effort. To achieve the best results and a successful outcome, you need to invest time, energy, and self-reflection. Sometimes, the uncertainty surrounding therapy can make you feel like you're wandering aimlessly and not making progress. In the worst case, it might even cause you to prematurely end your treatment, missing out on the benefits of therapy and the positive changes it can bring to your life. On the other hand, not having a clear plan can result in staying in therapy for an extended period without experiencing real progress.

So, here's how to make the most of your therapy sessions—a balance of spontaneous exploration and focused reflection.

1. Start with Admin Tasks

Before delving into your deepest thoughts, handle any administrative matters. It's best not to interrupt a breakthrough to write a check or schedule your next appointment. Address payment, scheduling, and insurance questions at the beginning of your first session. If you routinely check in with your therapist about any outstanding issues, you won't fall behind on payments or forget to schedule your next session.

2. Let Your Emotions Flow

In therapy, there's no need to hold back. With the right therapist, you should feel comfortable expressing your emotions. It's true that not everything will spill out at the start of your treatment. Trust-building takes time, even in the best therapist-patient matches. However, when you do feel at ease, let all your emotions into your sessions. While therapy often aims to address pain, frustration, and conflict, it's equally essential to share your moments of joy, success, and triumph.

Understanding what works well in your life is just as vital for self-discovery as recognizing your challenges. Focusing on the positive can be enlightening and may reveal the roots of negative behaviors. In general, be open to containing your feelings and examining them thoughtfully without letting emotions overwhelm you. In therapy, you learn to experience emotions without them taking over.

3. Keep the Focus on Yourself

As much as possible, try to keep the spotlight on yourself. It's easy to spend an entire therapy session venting about other people in your life or discussing unrelated circumstances. Venting and seeking third-party feedback are healthy and beneficial. However, real self-progress is challenging to achieve if you don't use your therapy sessions to explore yourself. Many people find it uncomfortable to talk about their feelings or themselves, and shifting the focus away from the self is common in therapy. To make the most of your sessions, keep the conversation centered on your own experiences.

4. Choose the Right Therapist

Ask yourself: What type of therapist do I need? Selecting the right therapist is crucial for making the most of your sessions. Effective treatment requires a therapist you can trust. Finding the right therapist involves some research and interviewing multiple candidates before making a decision.

Consider factors such as the therapist's gender, location, experience in dealing with specific issues, treatment methods, and insurance coverage. We already talked about how to choose the right therapist in the previous chapter.

5. Build a Trusting Connection

After choosing the right therapist, it's time to establish a trusting connection. Building trust should not be rushed; it takes time to open up emotionally. Just like any relationship, a strong therapeutic bond is developed, not discovered. To foster this connection, try to communicate directly with your therapist.

Keep in mind that no therapist is flawless. Therefore, it's essential to express what's working and what isn't during your sessions. You're paying for a service, and if you're dissatisfied, don't hesitate to voice your concerns. Evaluate what your therapist does well and where there's room for improvement. Do they need to explore new therapy techniques? Are there aspects missing from your sessions that you had hoped to address? Asking these questions can help you form a solid connection with your therapist.

6. Keep the Lines of Communication Open

It's a good idea to evaluate how your therapist interacts with you. You might want to consider their demeanor: Are they distant or too invasive? Do they challenge you appropriately, or is it too much? Is their tone off-putting? Do they come across as judgmental? Perhaps you worry about getting too attached or dependent on your therapist. Don't hesitate to speak up. This direct communication not only assists your therapist in helping you but also encourages you to step outside your comfort zone.

7. Do Regular Check-Ins

In addition to handling administrative tasks at the start of each session, make it a habit to check in with your therapist regularly. How's everything going? Are you satisfied with your progress? Did something your therapist said bother you a few weeks ago, but you never mentioned it? Are your session times still convenient for your schedule? This should be a two-way conversation where both you and your therapist share your thoughts. Having these periodic discussions, roughly once a month, can help prevent potential issues, accelerate your progress, and keep you engaged in the treatment.

8. Don't Stick Around in an Unfulfilling Relationship

If you've gone through multiple check-ins, candid conversations, and given the relationship time, but still don't feel aligned with the right therapist, it might be time to move on. If you don't feel emotionally vulnerable with your therapist, genuine progress in your treatment can be challenging. The worst mistake is not addressing discomfort or concerns with your therapist. It's normal to be hesitant to question or challenge your therapist, considering their authority. However, remember that they are mental health professionals who should be able to handle negative feedback. If your therapist doesn't respond well, it's a sign that you should consider exploring other options. Recognizing the signs of a good therapist is crucial for the overall impact of your treatment. A competent therapist will be open to taking responsibility for misunderstandings or missteps.

Some individuals remain with an ill-suited therapist for too long. Trust your instincts! If you're not comfortable or making progress, don't hesitate to discuss your concerns or end therapy. Advocate for yourself and actively participate in the treatment process. You have the right to discontinue treatment at any time, with no obligation except to pay for services received. If you've had a negative experience with counseling, it means you haven't found the right fit.

9. Seek Out Recurring Themes and Patterns

As you progress through your treatment, it's important not only to focus on each individual session but also to look for overarching themes and patterns. Therapy becomes most effective when we can connect the dots between events and gain insight into how our personalities and responses impact our well-being. These patterns help you gain a deeper understanding of how you operate in different situations, and this understanding will continue to serve you after your therapy journey ends and you navigate life independently. While your therapist will help you recognize these underlying themes and patterns related to the events you discuss, you can also actively search for them.

10. Share the Uncomfortable Thoughts

When it comes to therapy, it's not just about showing up; it's about opening up. This means being willing to discuss all those strange, uncomfortable thoughts that you might keep to yourself in other situations. In therapy, there's a welcoming space for unusual and odd thoughts. So, if you experience a sudden impulse or a peculiar memory crosses your mind, don't hesitate to bring it up. If you notice your sessions drifting into mere recaps of your week, or if you're unsure about what to discuss, try to dig deeper or revisit the initial reasons that led you to seek therapy in the first place. Ask yourself what you've been avoiding talking about and tackle it. Delve into self-discovery, exploring who you are, what you're feeling, and the reasons behind your actions.

11. Embrace Change and Be Ready for It

Many people seek therapy with the desire for significant life changes but may find it challenging when change actually begins to happen. To make the most of your therapy sessions, you should be prepared to accept that if you're seeking change, it often entails more transformations than you initially expected.

12. Extend the Work Beyond Your Sessions

If you're wondering how long therapy takes, it's important to understand that therapy is an ongoing process. It doesn't only occur during the one-hour weekly session with your therapist. As a client, you should continue your work outside these sessions and apply what you've learned to your daily life. This could involve specific tasks, such as taking steps towards a new career or making amends in a strained relationship. It could also mean making broader commitments to modify your behavior, like facing situations that trigger anxiety rather than avoiding them. Meditation, exercise, support groups, community involvement, and creative pursuits can all assist in bringing the changes you've discussed in your therapy sessions to life.

13. Embrace the Journey

Therapy involves a lot of effort, but it's not without its moments of joy. A breakthrough can feel like a huge weight being lifted off your shoulders. Think of therapy as enrolling in a course where you are the subject matter. If you put in the work, pay attention, and have a great teacher in your therapist, you're bound to make progress. Opening up to a stranger about the most private aspects of your life and mind can feel daunting, especially if you tend to keep your feelings close to your chest. In those moments, you might find yourself questioning, "Is my therapist judging me? Do I even need therapy for my anxiety? Am I crazy for being here?"

What To Not Say to Your Therapist

It's essential to understand that when we talk about "things you shouldn't say. However, there are certain statements that might hinder the therapeutic process, as outlined below.

1. *"I Agree with You Completely."*

Expressing sentiments like "You're so smart!", "I agree with you completely!"   can in a way affect the therapeutic experience. Therapy should be a secure space for engaging with authenticity and candor. From a therapist's perspective, it means a lot when a client voices concerns about the therapy environment or the therapist's approach because it offers an opportunity for adjustments to better support the client. This shows the client's investment in the therapeutic process and indicates progress toward creating a safe space where they can work through disagreements. Essentially, if you believe there are ways your therapist could enhance their support for you, don't hesitate to speak up.

2. *"That's What You Would Have Done, right?"*

Questions like, "You agree with me, don't you?" or you would have done the same right? are also counterproductive. There is a need for therapy to remain a safe space for genuine and honest engagement—it should work both ways. While it might not always be easy to accept your therapist's insights, it's vital to approach the process with an openness to at least consider their observations and insights. This requires embracing vulnerability with someone you likely haven't had much time to establish trust with, yet it's an essential part of building that trust in the therapeutic journey.

3. *"Tell Me What I Should Do."*

Therapy is all about empowerment. Statements such as, "Therapy will never work for someone like me," "I'm hopeless, this is pointless," or "Tell me what I should do," can be quite detrimental. It's crucial to understand that even though many individuals might feel shattered after experiencing traumas, difficulties, disappointments, or losses, it doesn't mean they are beyond repair. Therapy is, once again, a collaborative effort. You have to believe that underneath that feeling of brokenness, you are capable and resilient. The proof is in your survival, no matter the choices that were made to support you during and after these challenges. While acknowledging what you've been through is essential, allowing those experiences to hinder your progress is doing a disservice to yourself.

Chapter 5
When is It Time to End Therapy?

Starting therapy is a significant step, and your connection with your therapist becomes a pivotal part of your life. Your therapy sessions might even become a top priority, crucial for your well-being and your ability to manage other life commitments – **but this isn't meant to be a never-ending journey.**

The main aim of therapy is to help you gain insights and develop tools to effectively deal with the issues that led you to therapy in the first place. However, there's no set duration for this process, no final test to pass, and no official graduation ceremony to mark the end of therapy. Although your therapist can offer guidance, the decision to conclude therapy and the timing of that decision are ultimately in your hands.

So, how long should therapy really last? Research suggests that for many people, a range of 15 to 20 therapy sessions is often ideal. But remember, this can vary widely. The duration depends on multiple factors, including the complexity of the issues you're addressing, your specific therapy goals, your connection with your therapist, and most importantly, your commitment to achieving those goals.

Therapy is more than just showing up to your sessions or having a confidant to talk to, although that's a part of it. Successful therapy requires you to put in effort beyond the therapy room – reflecting on your therapist's advice, applying the skills you've learned, and sometimes doing additional work like reading books or keeping journals as assigned by your therapist. The timeline and the success of your therapy largely depend on your active involvement.

Starting with the End in Mind

The decision to conclude therapy isn't a last-minute thing. It's a process that actually begins from your very first sessions with your therapist. In those initial meetings, you'll likely get a sense of whether you want to establish an ongoing therapeutic relationship.

Right from your first session, you can start asking some important questions, both to your therapist and to yourself, which will guide the entire process:

What are the specific goals I aim to achieve through therapy? (It might be useful to write these down to revisit later.)

Is there an estimated timeline for my therapy journey?

Will we regularly assess and discuss my progress?

Will you provide guidance on when it might be time to conclude therapy?

Recognizing the Signs of Closure

Deciding to end therapy doesn't usually happen overnight. It's a gradual progression, and you'll likely notice some signs along the way, indicating that the time may be approaching:

You've successfully achieved the goals you set when you first began therapy.

The symptoms or issues that brought you to therapy have notably improved, and you generally feel better.

You find yourself having less to talk about with your therapist than before.

You believe you now have the skills and tools to handle the problems you initially sought therapy for.

Your therapist agrees that you've made significant progress and are ready to conclude therapy.

On the other hand, there are scenarios where you might opt to end therapy for less positive reasons. It could be that you've found therapy unhelpful, the therapist isn't the right fit for your specific needs, or you're not comfortable with them. There's also the possibility that you're not fully prepared for the therapy process. Life events or other commitments might make it challenging for you to continue therapy at this moment. If your schedule or personal commitment to the work outside of your sessions is a challenge, it could be worth considering concluding therapy and revisiting it when you're fully ready.

Are You Ready to Say Goodbye?

If you sense that the end of therapy is approaching, work collaboratively with your therapist to figure out the right time and prepare for the transition. Your therapist might initiate this discussion when they feel you're ready. It's important to review the progress you've made during your therapy journey, go over the skills you've acquired, and discuss how to apply them in your life moving forward.

If you struggle with ending relationships or farewells, talk about this with your therapist. Unless your therapist is retiring, moving, or unable to continue sessions, you can inquire about scheduling less frequent sessions instead of ending them abruptly. Also, explore the possibility of returning for occasional check-ins if new issues arise in your life. Even if therapy is concluding for now, it doesn't mean it can't restart when or if you need it in the future.

Conclusion

Embracing The Beauty of Therapy

In the depths of the human experience, we often find ourselves entangled in the complexities of our own minds and hearts. Throughout this book, we've embarked on a journey to explore the profound beauty of therapy, a journey that has taken us into the depths of self-discovery. We've witnessed the power of dialogue, the gift of vulnerability, and the extraordinary capacity for growth that lies within each of us. As we reach the conclusion of this exploration, it is fitting to reflect on the profound importance of therapy in our lives.

Therapy, as we've discovered, is not a sign of weakness but a testament to our resilience. It is not an admission of failure, but a declaration of our commitment to personal growth and well-being. The beauty of therapy lies in its ability to provide a safe and supportive space for self-reflection, self-acceptance, and self-improvement. It is an oasis of healing where we can confront our fears, untangle the knots of our past, and chart a path towards a more authentic and fulfilling existence.

Throughout this book, we've delved into the many ways therapy can empower individuals to break free from the shackles of mental and emotional anguish. We've celebrated the therapist-client relationship, a partnership founded on trust and understanding that often becomes the catalyst for profound change.

But why should everyone consider talking to a therapist at some point in their lives? The answer is as simple as it is profound. Just as our bodies require occasional medical check-ups to ensure good health, our minds and emotions deserve a periodic examination as well. We all face moments of confusion, pain, and despair, and at these junctures, a therapist can serve as our guide, offering a lantern in the darkness, a compass for the lost, and a lifeline for the drowning.

The beauty of therapy extends to every facet of our existence. It is the compass that can guide us through life's uncertain terrain, helping us navigate storms with grace and resilience. Therapy is the sanctuary where we confront our deepest fears and insecurities and learn to embrace our true selves with compassion and acceptance.

At the heart of therapy is the idea that we are not alone in our struggles. It provides a space where the whispers of our pain are heard, where our stories are met with empathy, and where our tears are transformed into stepping stones towards personal growth. Through therapy, we gain the insight to understand the origins of our patterns and the tools to reshape our narratives. It empowers us to make conscious choices, foster healthier relationships, and cultivate the life we desire.

Therapy is a gift we bestow upon ourselves, an investment in our own well-being and happiness. It is a testament to our courage and a recognition of our worthiness. No matter our background, experiences, or the burdens we carry, therapy invites us to unburden our hearts and minds, to heal, and to embark on a journey of self-discovery.

So, I encourage to embrace the beauty of therapy in your own life. Whether you're currently navigating the turbulent waters of mental health challenges or simply seeking personal growth, therapy can be a beacon of hope, and a source of resilience and transformation.

Remember that seeking help is not a sign of weakness but a manifestation of your strength. Each of us has the capacity for healing, growth, and fulfillment, and therapy is a remarkable tool to aid us on this remarkable journey.

As we conclude this exploration, may we remember that we are not alone on this path, and that the beauty of therapy is a reminder of our shared humanity and our endless potential for growth and self-discovery.

In the embrace of therapy, we find the courage to confront our shadows, the strength to heal our wounds, and the wisdom to embrace the fullness of our lives. So, take that step, make that appointment, and embark on the journey of a lifetime. The beauty of therapy awaits you, ready to unlock the boundless potential that resides within.

www.ingramcontent.com/pod-product-compliance
Lightning Source LLC
Chambersburg PA
CBHW050838260726
48660CB00006B/2320